# *Tails from SC CARES*

by
Cindy Hedrick

## Tails from SC CARES
by Cindy Hedrick

Copyright © 2021

All rights reserved.

In accordance with the U.S. Copyright Act of 1976, the scanning, uploading and electronic sharing of any part of this book without the permission of the publisher is unlawful piracy and theft of the author's intellectual property. If you would like to use material from the book (other than for review purposes), prior written permission must be obtained by contacting the publisher.

Photographs from the author's personal collection.

ISBN 978-1-950768-67-7

Published in the United States by
CLASS
Publishing Division
P.O. Box 2884
Pawleys Island, SC 29585
www.ClassAtPawleys.com

*It is man's sympathy with all
creatures that first makes him
truly a man.
Until he extends his circle of
compassion to all living things,
man will not himself find peace.*

*Dr. Albert Schweitzer
Nobel Peace Prize, 1952*

## *Dedication*

*To the wonderful creatures we were fortunate to share our lives with and the humans who grew to love them! What an amazing journey!*

*To my soulmate, Skip Yeager, who shared in this dream and vision and is the one who made it all possible!*

*To all of the volunteers and donors who made this place possible for so many years!*

*To my grandchildren, Emma, James and John, along with all the children who might enjoy this book! My hope is that it brings you a connection to the animals we share our planet with, so that your compassion for their well-being grows strong!*

## *Chapters*

| | | |
|---|---|---|
| Introduction | | 1 |
| 1 | Savannah | 7 |
| 2 | The Meaning of Fortitude | 12 |
| 3 | Kindred Spirits | 17 |
| 4 | Birds of a Feather | 24 |
| 5 | Don't Give Up | 32 |
| 6 | Friends of Feather and Fur | 36 |
| 7 | Have You Ever Hugged a Turkey? | 41 |
| 8 | Missy's Amazing Recovery | 46 |
| 9 | Our Little Dinosaurs | 52 |
| 10 | Sassy | 59 |
| 11 | We Are All Important | 65 |
| 12 | Wolf Pack | 71 |
| 13 | A Cat Named "Mayo" | 80 |
| Words and their Definitions | | 84 |
| Sanctuaries and Acknowledgment | | 86 |

## Introduction

**SC CARES – SC Coastal Animal Rescue & Educational Sanctuary** was open for 13 years caring for exotics, farm animals and non-releasable wildlife. The journey was intense but extremely rewarding, giving sanctuary to close to 200 animals at a given time. In addition to the animals, we were fortunate to meet many like-minded compassionate humans who grew to love the creatures as we did. Educational tours met our secondary mission which was to help people connect to these sentient creatures and begin to care about their well-being. Over the 13 years we hosted tours for thousands of people from all over.

*How it all began*

Early on I volunteered for our local humane society assisting in animal cruelty calls, and always had dogs, cats and even a horse at one point. Rescue was in my DNA. After meeting Skip, we decided to take wildlife rehabilitation classes where we learned how to care for infant and injured wildlife. We focused on opossums, squirrels and raptors. In joining this group, we helped work a hot-line for incoming calls, and much to our amazement there were many calls about surrendering exotic animals. Like many of our colleagues, we began to take these exotics into our homes since there was nowhere else for them to go. After a year or so, we had taken in parrots, prairie dogs, sugar gliders, iguanas and even a snake. It soon became clear as we continued to receive calls to help exotics, a place for these types of animals to find refuge was needed – an idea was born!

After researching, planning and trying to make the best decisions possible we found a sweet spot in Georgetown, S.C., away from most humans but we had hoped close enough to Charleston and Myrtle Beach to attract visitors and volunteers. We sold everything, two houses and two businesses, to make this transition possible. We officially moved to Georgetown in 2006 with 36 animals we had previously taken in. The property had a 900 square foot cabin where we lived with our dogs. We constructed an 1800 square foot Quonset hut to house indoor residents and began building fences for outdoor animals. We used some of the proceeds from the sale of our properties to purchase a small candy store, known as Sweeties, in Georgetown so we would have some personal income. Skip was the primary manager of the store and took the business to many lengths beyond what it was when we purchased it. We have not gotten wealthy from it, but thankfully it has paid our bills.

Operating a non-profit animal sanctuary was all-consuming, and with no guidance we had no idea of the time and energy it would take. Caring for the animals daily was a full-time job and my primary concern.

Within the first couple of years, we had taken in more animals and thankfully met some people who were coming out to volunteer to help us. It took no time at all to be overwhelmed, even with being incredibly careful about which animals we thought we could help; there were just so many we had to turn away. It was heartbreaking every time we said "no," but we had to try to survive for those we already had.

Our entire lives were devoted to SC CARES. We worked tirelessly to keep it going. Early mornings for me were filled with bookkeeping, correspondence, fundraising efforts, grant writing, ordering food, and research – then more research. I was constantly trying to learn more and more about how to give these creatures the best lives we could offer them. Once the day had started, it was feeding and cleaning for the animals, training and managing volunteers, hosting tours in the afternoon, then evening feeding for those animals that ate twice a day.

Skip's primary goals were not only to run our candy store but also buy materials and handle construction which was a constant need. Building fences was only a small part of it; housing for each animal had to be done as well. Barns were built as well as huts for the outside animals. His masterpiece was the wolf den with a waterfall feature that recycled water to two other compounds for wolf hybrids. Thankfully, we did have several construction volunteers that made it all possible, but Skip was the designer, purchaser of materials and lead builder, so his life was also overwhelming.

I must take this opportunity to mention a very special volunteer, Captain Homer Winter, retired Navy fighter pilot, who read about our need for help constructing a barn for a horse we had taken in. He made the call to come help and once he did, he never left. He was an amazing human being at 85 years of age, was in extremely good shape, and worked so hard building so many of our construction needs, in addition to food pickups and trash hauls. He also helped keep us afloat financially for the nine years he was with us. Hank, as he preferred to be called, was at the sanctuary six days a week from nine o'clock in the morning until six o'clock in the evening. He would sit with me under the trees at the end of the day and we would talk about anything and everything. He became one of my dearest friends.

When Hank passed at age 94, we held a memorial service here, which was the only service of any kind that he requested, and we laid his ashes to rest in the graveyard with the animals. Hank told me many times in our talks that he had told his family he did not want a funeral and being buried here was all he wanted. He even asked me to bury one of our hounds, when he passed, with him, which we did when the time came. There were 30 or more volunteers who came out for his service, in addition to his favorite dog and the horse that brought him here years ago. He was truly an angel for SC CARES and what an inspiration to all he met!

Over the years things began to be a little easier. At least there were set routines, schedules and veteran volunteers. In 2015, a grey cloud came over us. Skip was diagnosed with multiple myeloma, bone cancer which is incurable at this point in time. He survived a stem cell transplant in that same year and, so far, is doing well except for loss of energy from the drugs he has to take. Every three months his blood is tested to make sure the cancer cells are not climbing. Every time I wait with fear to hear the results. This concern really took its toll on me with the fear of losing him and how I, alone, could ever manage what we had built. In addition to this major concern, I was constantly worried about funding and help, not to mention the awful hurricanes we had endured. I suppose it was just too overwhelming for me as my and Skip's bodies were already weary from working 24/7 for 365 days a year for 13 years.

To me, the future looked dark and, although I struggled to think of answers to all these issues, I could not seem to find anything to make this work. So, rather than things deteriorating slowly and, with my concern for the animals' well-being, I felt it best to think about closing and hopefully finding other great sanctuaries where our animals could go. This was by far the most heartbreaking decision I had ever made in my entire life and one that I struggled to convince Skip of for months. He is always more optimistic than I, while I am the realist considering all the factors. He finally gave in and I started reaching out to place our animals.

For the next year, my life was filled with transporting animals myself, or arranging transport for the animals for whom we had found new sanctuary. During my first transport, I cried all the way there and all the way back, and my heart broke each and every time I had to say goodbye to these innocent creatures I had promised to care for for the rest of my life! Would they be okay and be happy? Would they ever forgive me? How could I help them understand? It took us from April 2019 to February 2020 to place all the animals, which is exceptionally good considering most good sanctuaries are always at capacity.

I must believe that our higher power had something to do with our good fortune which brings me to why I wrote this book. Although physically SC CARES has ended, I wanted to share with others just a few of the incredible creatures we met on this journey, and how much alike humans and animals are. I hope you enjoy meeting them and find it in your heart to love all creatures with whom we share our planet. As Albert Schweitzer says: "Until he extends his circle of compassion to include all living things, man will not himself find peace."

Sincerely and, as always, for the animals!
Cindy Hedrick & Skip Yeager,
Founders and Directors
of SC CARES

Savannah, Blue & Gold Macaw, naked and the heart of SC Cares.

# 1
## *Savannah*

These stories are meant to inspire others to realize that animals are sentient beings, who during their lifetimes can suffer from trauma through difficult circumstances, and carry with them emotional scars and psychological issues, just as people do. This brings me to Savannah, the inspiration for SC CARES.

Prior to opening SC CARES in 2006, Skip and I worked with a Wildlife Rehab group in North Carolina. Unfortunately, it was not just native wildlife we received calls for. There were so many exotic animal calls that many of us, as volunteers, had started taking some of these creatures that had nowhere to go into our homes. This need is what created the concept of SC CARES.

One call came from Animal Control asking if we could help with a Blue & Gold Macaw that had been confiscated by the officers due to animal abuse. Apparently, a family had separated and were preparing to divorce. After a custody battle, the mother obtained custody of the children, but no one wanted the macaw. The father was stuck with the bird, upset about losing his children, and he took his distraught emotions out on the bird. According to the report filed by a neighbor, he put the Blue & Gold Macaw in the dark basement, barely keeping her alive. When she would call out, as parrots will do when they want/need attention, he would throw items down the stairs at the cage, or go to the cage yelling at the bird to shut up and shake it, which is called "earthquaking," and even took a spray bottle with the sprayer on stream to squirt the parrot, which was painful to our thin-skinned feather friend. Due to lack of positive attention, being alone and stressed from the abuse, Savannah began to pull her feathers out. No charges were filed against this man for animal abuse on the condition he give up the bird to the authorities, which of course he eagerly agreed to do as he did not want the parrot. It is sad that animal abuse occurs for any creature but even worse for these exotics that most people do not understand to begin with.

Macaws are the largest parrots in the exotic "pet bird" industry. Found in the wild in Central and

Savannah after a shower with special shampoo, hopefully to help her stop plucking.

Savannah's back and wings missing feathers.

*Savannah*

Savannah, asking for a pet from Cindy.

South America, these magnificent creatures have been captured and bred to produce profits for the pet bird industry. Macaws have the capability to be very loud, very destructive and potentially extremely dangerous. With a bite pressure of close to 300 pounds per square inch (300 psi), they could bite your finger off, bone and all. Living with a macaw is like having a loud 3-year-old toddler for 80 to 100 years, which is their lifespan. Parrots are very social creatures in need of friendship, stimulation to reduce boredom, and space to play. Parrots will self-mutilate by plucking their feathers out, similar to nervous conditions that we as humans suffer from, such as nail biting or hair-pulling. Parrots often will not stop at feather plucking but will mutilate the skin as well, which is even more critical and leads to infection and sometimes death. It is sad that Savannah was so upset that she would pull out her own feathers, leaving the very thin skin vulnerable. After some time, feather plucking will cause the follicle to simply close and no new feather growth will occur ever again. After taking Savannah in, our paperwork showed that she was hatched in 1956, making her 57 years old and the eldest macaw at SC CARES. This also means that the previous family she lived with was more than likely a second or third home for her. Savannah has stopped plucking, so thankfully she is not causing any further damage to her body. Savannah was most definitely an inspiration to us to create the sanctuary known as SC CARES.

Savannah saying "hello" from a branch above our heads.
This is how her body will look for the rest of her life.

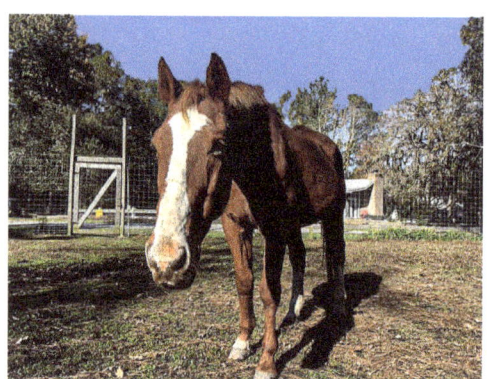

Fortitude – now safe, fed and loved.

# 2
# *The Meaning of Fortitude*

Fortitude implies not only patience, but courage and strength of character during pain, affliction, or hardship.

This is a story about a horse we named Fortitude and called him Forty for short. His life started out okay, but Forty had lived with several different humans before his 23rd birthday. Those homes were good, but as he aged and did not perform for the humans as well as they wanted, they moved him to someone else. This sadly happens to many horses, as they are sold and traded around throughout their lifetimes.

This "home" was not like any of the other places he had lived. He did not have a barn or shelter, nor a fenced in area to roam, but instead was tied on a rope to a stake that kept him from moving around much at all. The area he was tied in was marshy with mostly weeds he could not eat. He was near a dirty pond which was supposed to be his water source. The people who lived there would come and go, but no one would go out to

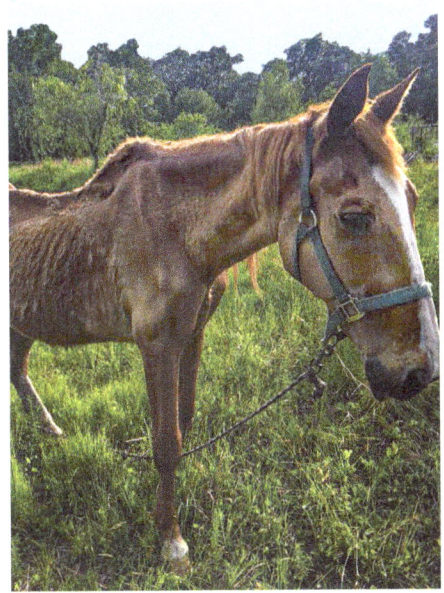 

Fortitude, literally on his last leg, near total starvation; tied out with no shelter, no food or any clean water.

give this poor horse some food and clean water! I feel sure Forty wondered what he had done to deserve this life! This abuse and neglect are unforgivable to a creature who cannot help himself.

Forty had to stand there in the same spot, with the sun beating down on him and no shade, bugs constantly biting him, and was drenched when it rained. In cold temps he also stood there, no shelter to block the cold wind, and no way to keep warm. This horrible life went on for him for two years. Honestly, we were shocked he had even survived it!

After being notified of this poor creature's existence, we planned to go get him. We had to call the Sheriff's Department to meet us there, since we wanted no trouble with taking him away from this horror. When we arrived, my eyes swelled with tears and my stomach felt sick. Forty came right to us and I felt that I could hear him saying, "Thank you, thank you, for saving me!" His poor body was a wreck, so frail, weak, and malnourished. He was covered in fungus that caused him to itch constantly. He had patches of hair left from his winter coat that had not been brushed, and this was in June! Also knots were all through his mane, and his hooves needed work as did his teeth.

Forty mustered what strength he had left to get on the trailer, but then jumped off when we arrived because he could see and hear other horses. I am sure he was very lonely in addition to everything else. Horses

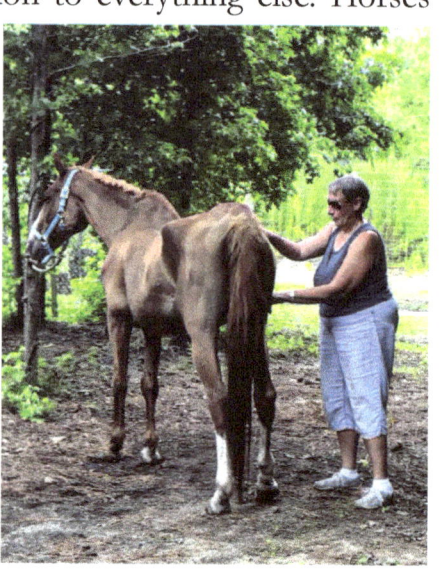

(Right) Carole Miller, our equine massage therapist, helping Fortitude feel better.

(Lower left) Fortitude as we found him, tied to a stake in the weeds, near a murky pond – pitiful!

(Lower right) Cindy and Fortitude doing an interview for a local TV station on his horrific abuse.

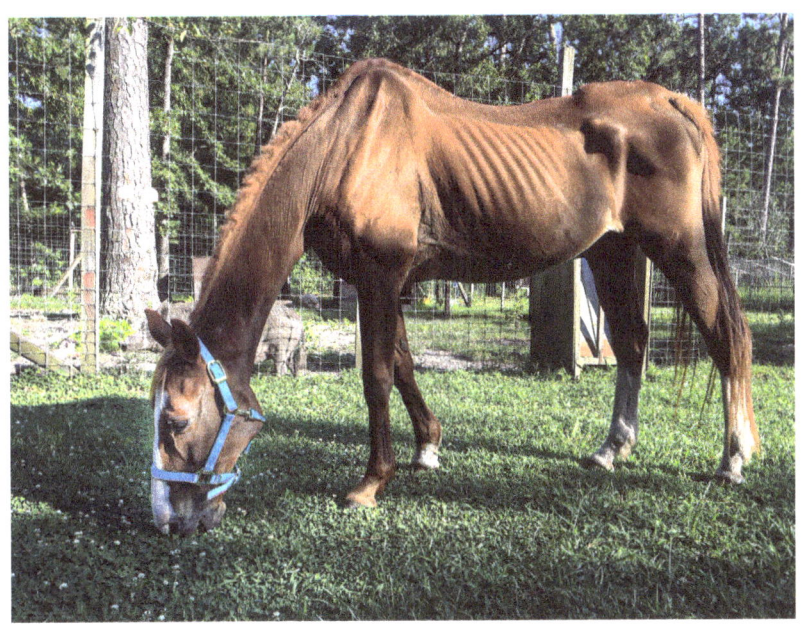

Fortitude after he started putting on a little weight.

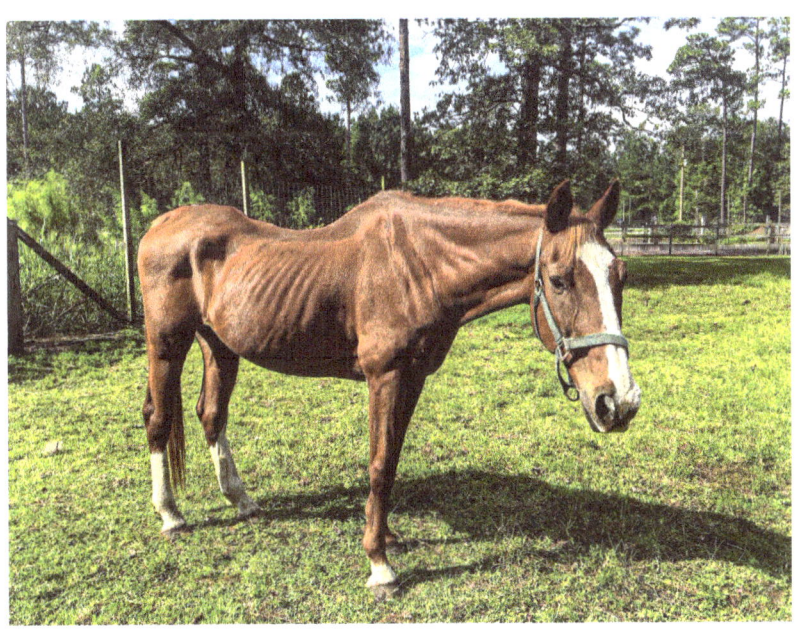

like to be with herds, their herds are their families. We got Forty settled in for the night in an area with grass and clover where he could roam, and fresh clean water and a little food and hay to get him started on his road to recovery.

In the days that followed we bathed him, brushed him, applied medicine and fed him small amounts of food several times a day. The vet came out to check on him regularly as he continued to gain strength. Forty could roam even more of the property and became quite the character! He would try to help himself to groceries as we were putting them away, and even opened the door to one of the buildings and went inside – that was a sight to see! Once inside, he opened one of the food containers, turned it over and had a buffet!

In this story of Fortitude something happened that I will never forget. His first night here I was worried he might be scared in a new place, so I took a flashlight and went out to check on him. He did look a little startled, but I went to him and began stroking him and telling him he was all right now, and he would never have to be hungry, lonely or scared ever again. I reached up and put my arms around his neck to hug him, and he instantly put his head around my neck to hug me back. We stood there for a few seconds, embracing and sharing our love for each other. I knew he was grateful to be safe and loved.

As humans we forget that we are not the only ones who "feel" things; animals have feelings too! Always remember that!

Star and Ghost – best friends.

## 3
## *Kindred Spirits*

This is a story of two wounded souls who miraculously found each other, healed each other, and became kindred spirits. SC CARES is only the vehicle that allowed this to happen – the wolves are the champions in this by forgiving us humans and making themselves whole again.

So, to begin – Star is a wolf that had been chained to a tree for all her life, approximately five years. No one had ever shown kindness, love or respect to this magnificent creature. Through a raid by the authorities, this wolf was confiscated but we declined to take her and searched for other rescues that might possibly help, but to no avail. The officer was persistent since he knew

Star being transferred to us by animal control.

Star riding with us back to the sanctuary, terrified and scared.

Star in her enclosure at the sanctuary, happy and loved.

she would be put down if she had nowhere to go, so to save her life, we found a way to take her in. On our two-hour journey back to SC CARES, Skip and I were both shedding tears for all that she had been through, how terrified she was, and the fact that we almost did not take her. We felt guilty for all the others we had turned away, but making it possible for her reminded us of the Starfish poem (printed at the end of this chapter). We may not have been able to help all those who needed us, but helping her made all the difference in her world. This poem is why we gave her the name "Star." We kept talking to her in a quiet, calm manner, trying to comfort her fears. When we arrived and placed her in a secure sheltered area, we were amazed to see her timidly approach us. We could sense that she meant us no harm, and our friendship began. Within minutes, she was licking our faces and allowing us to hug her! I could feel her gratitude for the love we offered her. All it took was a little compassion!

Then one day, several years after Star's arrival, we received a call for a young, neutered male, high content wolf hybrid. At first, we declined to take him, as we had turned away other wolves and wolf hybrids, thinking that Star would not tolerate another animal in her area. Star had displayed intolerance of the other canines at SC CARES. We could not risk upsetting her now that she was happy. When we received a second call from the young lady trying to place him, we went a step further and checked with our wolf advisor about the possibility of these two cohabiting. Our advisor said this situation would most likely work for Star, if she accepted him and could be the dominant partner since she was older, and the area was established as hers.

Meet Ghost. At 8 months old, SC CARES was to be his fourth home. Ghost is an extremely high content wolf hybrid that had been sold by a wolf breeder in California. He arrived very skittish of humans, even terrified of men, so I began to work with him. After some weeks we finally formed a bond; he would allow me to walk him, pet him, and even give him kisses. We introduced him to Star, and they seemed immediately infatuated with each other, almost as if they had been waiting to meet! They played and had so much fun together.

Ghost on his outing to visit with Star.

We were almost ready to move them in together when a tragedy occurred ... the neighboring full-blooded wolf pack attacked Ghost under the fence (something we didn't realize was even possible with a fence and covering to the ground). Ghost was injured and terrified and who could blame him? Thankfully, after many weeks, his physical injuries healed, but psychologically he was once again let down by a human (me) ... our bond was damaged. My heart was breaking for this poor creature. I wondered how I could ever walk him back to Star's compound when he would not even allow me to touch him. Skip continued to take Star to his shelter to visit; they acted like long-lost friends reunited each time. While Star was with him, Ghost would watch her let me love her and exchange hugs, and he began to come to me, skeptical, but he did approach. Star's trust in me gave him the confidence to give me another chance. After several of these visits, I was finally able to pet him and eventually put his collar on again.

On to the happy ending – we were able to move Ghost into Star's habitat and now the two of them run,

Star and Ghost playing, but look at those teeth!

Ghost and Star tired after playing.

Star and Ghost cooling off and getting a drink.

play, and wrestle. We are confident that their friendship will bring them much happiness, and together they will continue to thrive. For two creatures whose future was once dismal, we are so thankful we could help their stories have a different ending! This is what sanctuaries live for ... it is amazing what a little love, kindness and respect will do. Once again, the forgiving nature and ability to trust again is a trait these animals have that we humans could learn from.

### The Starfish Story

An old man was walking on the beach one morning after a storm. In the distance, he could see someone moving like a dancer. As he came closer, he saw that it was a young woman picking up starfish and gently throwing them into the ocean.

"Young lady, why are you throwing starfish into the ocean?"

"The sun is up, and the tide is going out, and if I do not throw them in, they will die," she said.

"But, young lady, do you not realize that there are many miles of beach and thousands of starfish? You cannot possibly make a difference."

The young woman listened politely, then bent down, picked up another starfish, and threw it into the sea.

"It made a difference for that one."

~ *Adapted from the original by Loren Eiseley*

Geronimo – Catalina Macaw

# 4
# *Birds of a Feather*

SC CARES was home to over 150 animals at any given time and more than 50 of those animals were birds, parrots to be precise! Parrots ranging from tiny little parakeets to very large macaws! This story is about Geronimo, one of the macaws. Geronimo is a hybrid macaw, meaning a man-made species not found in the wild, and referred to as a Catalina. Unfortunately, parrots like Geronimo are being bred and sold in pet stores and through private breeders. They sell for close to $1,000 each, and that was Geronimo's beginning.

When Geronimo arrived at SC CARES, he was only 5 years old, which is still a baby for parrots that live 80-100 years. The most horrifying part of this is that SC CARES was his fifth home! This poor bird had been sold, returned, sold again, placed in another home and passed to yet another home. All these changes in his environment, housing, and the people he was introduced to caused him to be a very angry bird. Thankfully, Geronimo isn't one of the birds that started plucking his feathers, like some of our other residents. Geronimo's coping mechanism was to bite. Who could blame him with what had happened to him. He no longer felt that he could trust humans, and that I completely understand. As his new caregivers, this was a very intimidating issue to deal with since a parrot's beak is SO strong, they can bite your finger off or tear down your house bit by bit if allowed to roam freely!

When Geronimo arrived, I'll admit I was intimidated for sure, but I could see how nervous and scared he was. He was trying to be tough, so that I couldn't see how truly terrified he really felt. Seeing this fear in his eyes gave me determination to prove to him that not all humans are bad, that I had compassion for him and what he had been through, and that I just wanted him to be happy, feel safe and enjoy his life in the best way possible. I had to be very careful working with him, his beak is very large and sharp, and he moves with rapid speed, and I prefer to keep all my ten fingers.

It was apparent after a few weeks that this misunderstood boy only wanted to be loved and accepted, and I was determined to give him just that! These macaws do talk, oftentimes repeating what they've heard, and Geronimo had quite a library of language; most of it profanity or ugly words like "shut up."

Geronimo asking if we have a treat.

Buzz and Geronimo
Always Together
Geronimo and Buzz

*Birds of a Feather*

This told me a lot about what his life had been like prior to us. I was horrified to think of the situations he must have been in. Geronimo would lunge at me and try to bite me and then let out some of the ugliest words you've ever heard, and I could picture how this scenario had played out. Working with abused and troubled parrots, it's been my experience that the less attention you pay to a bad habit, the quicker it will stop. Ignoring foul language and bad behavior is hard for us to do, but it really is the best thing to create an atmosphere of peace. These parrots are very intelligent and sensitive beings and seek attention, be it good or bad, so walking away from a lunging bird will stop the behavior much faster than trying to reason with them.

Of course, going back to show them loving attention is also key. They crave our attention and want to be noticed, so after walking away from negative behavior I would try going back and start singing and dancing with him. This turned out great! Geronimo is one of the first macaws that would start bobbing back and forth as I sang and danced for him. When we were playing music for the birds, and I started singing and dancing, there are lots of parrots who joined in. Some singing, some dancing and some doing both! I don't think any of us will end up on "America's Got Talent," and I'm sure it's quite a sight, but it's SO much fun!

Once we moved Geronimo into the aviary with the other macaws, he quickly took up with Buzz, a Harlequin macaw (also a hybrid) we had taken in. These two birds are inseparable, and you could see the bond they have is strong. They preened each other, fed each other and are together 24/7. On treat days at SC CARES, the parrots would be given grapes, apples, cherry tomatoes, broccoli, sugar snaps, or whatever we had an abundance of. Geronimo was most appreciative of his treats. I remember giving them cherry tomatoes; it was Geronimo's first treat day, and he let out a loud "UUMM" and wanted more. It was music to my ears to know he was happy!

Geronimo, although having had a rough start in his life, is one of the lucky ones, and I am so grateful to be part of the journey! Humans can be this way also! If someone you know is angry or grouchy, try giving them a little time and understanding and lots of love and, hopefully, they will change, too!

Buzz and Geronimo – Friends for life!

(Left) Geronimo – Catalina Macaw hybrid bred by a Blue & Gold Macaw and a Scarlet Macaw

(Center) Buzz – Harlequin Macaw hybrid bred by a Blue & Gold Macaw and a Green Wing Macaw

(Right) Jade – Military Macaw, a pure species found in the wild, although their population is decreasing due to poaching and loss of habitat

(Left to Right) Celeste (Blue & Gold Macaw), Geronimo (Catalina Macaw), Buzz (Harlequin Macaw), Jade (Military Macaw)

*Birds of a Feather*

Sweetie with the most beautiful eyes ever!

# 5
# *Don't Give Up*

Sweetie is a white-tailed deer who was born on a warm spring day. Like all fawns, she followed her mom so she could learn how to be a deer. Her mom was teaching her what to eat, places to go, how to hide and who to stay away from. It was a normal day when Sweetie was out with her mom, and suddenly a large dog appeared and began barking at them! Her mom signaled for her to run away, but as she did, Sweetie stepped into some tree roots and her leg became stuck! The dog continued to bark. Sweetie's heart was racing. The dog's human came to see what was happening and discovered Sweetie's predicament. He was very calm and gentle and only wanted to help her. He freed her leg and knew she needed help. He called the sanctuary to see if we could help her. Of course, we said YES!

When Sweetie arrived, her heart was beating so fast we feared it could be fatal. She was truly terrified! Thankfully, I had some calming herbs with me and was able to get her into a quiet small place and help her start to calm down. Wild infant deer are so afraid of humans that simply touching them could stress them out to the point of death. As she was settling down, we began bottle feeding her and she quickly came to like us. After a visit to the vet, it was determined that Sweetie had not broken anything in her leg but instead mangled all the tendons. With the leg twisted, it was causing her to fall when trying to stand. The vet suggested we amputate the leg to give her a better chance at a happy life, so we did.

Sweetie when she arrived with her leg twisted and mangled.

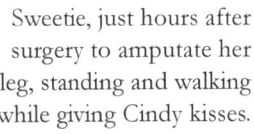

Sweetie, just hours after surgery to amputate her leg, standing and walking while giving Cindy kisses.

Her surgery went well. Within hours of being back at the sanctuary, she stood up and began to move around. As time went on, Sweetie grew bigger and stronger. We noticed a change in her body that was incredible. Her remaining back leg shifted so that now it was in the middle of her back, giving her complete balance! Sweetie lived with another deer that had all four legs, and she adapted so well to having one back leg that she could run faster than he could! Just remember, when life changes or somehow you're different, don't ever give up! Keep trying, do your best and you will succeed!

Sweetie getting ready to go eat breakfast.

Sweetie on three legs was still the fastest of them all!!
So beautiful.

*Don't Give Up*

Garfield, a truly amazing cat!

# 6
## *Friends of Feather and Fur*

This is a story of unique friendship between a bird and a cat! Many of you may have had the pleasure of living with a cat and a dog who got along in a loving family way. But when you think of cats and birds, getting along is not usually how you would see them. Garfield is an orange tabby who was found roaming the streets, and Snuggles is an Umbrella Cockatoo who came to live at the sanctuary. These two would form an amazing friendship that seemed to work for them.

I have to say I was concerned about how a cat living with birds could work out with no mishaps, but I was fortunate enough to see the transition take place. While living at the sanctuary, I came into what I feared would be a potential disaster. One of the Blue and Gold Macaws (the largest of parrots) was sneaking up behind Garfield, and as I watched, I thought about how to handle this.

Garfield was laying on the floor twitching his tail as cats often do, and the bird stood behind him curiously and gently touched his tail with his beak. It took Garfield a second or two to realize what was happening, but when he did, the two of them faced off! The bird was in a defensive posture, foot up, wings raised and beak open, while Garfield stood up with his paw in the air ready to swat!

It was intense for just a second, then I could almost hear the two animals saying to each other, "I guess we'll just let this go," as they both turned and walked away.

When Snuggles came into the sanctuary, Garfield had no idea what was about to take place. Snuggles is one of those parrots that LOVES attention from everyone! What a character she is! Snuggles gets her name honestly because snuggling is one of her favorite things to do! Full of personality, she never meets a stranger and believes everyone would enjoy her affection, and this included Garfield!

Snuggles is an Umbrella Cockatoo – lifespan averages 80 years.

*Friends of Feather and Fur*

Though Garfield slept in many place, Snuggles could always find him.

Here, Snuggles was using her foot to pet Garfield.

*Tails from SC CARES*

Garfield looks like he's thinking of what to say, while Snuggles waits for his response!

Snuggles loves to play with Garfield by attempting to "pet" him by preening (combing) his hair. Garfield is such a patient friend, allowing Snuggles to touch him with her beak and foot. When he's had enough of her advances, Garfield simply walks away. Often Snuggles will walk down the hall to try to catch up to him, but usually gives up when she realizes he's much faster than she is walking on the floor which, by the way, is a funny sight to see (a bird running behind a cat!).

Garfield and Snuggles are completely opposite creatures, but found a friendship despite their differences, teaching us that being different does not mean we cannot be friends!

Garfield and Snuggles, hanging out.

Jerry, our handsome boy!

# 7
# *Have You Ever Hugged a Turkey?*

SC CARES was open to helping all sorts of creatures, including a very friendly turkey! Jerry was a broad breasted male turkey whose feathers were so colorful and beautiful. The human who previously cared for him had a nice garden that Jerry roamed freely, grazing all day. This led to his extra weight and unfortunately caused other health issues.

Once Jerry was settled in at SC CARES, we discovered how friendly he was, following us around and calling out to us! He wanted attention and his hugs were the best! He was such a sweet boy and soon became the favorite of everyone, even visitors. Nearly

Cindy talking with Jerry and giving him some love.

everyone wanted to hug Jerry because he gave the best hugs! Often, he would lay his head on your shoulder that allowed him to hug you back, which was such a special feeling.

In the hot summer months Jerry would pant, yes, just like a dog.

Jerry cooling off in front of his fan.

We brought out a large barn fan and positioned it so he could stand in front of it to cool off. He also had a pool we encouraged him to stand in to cool down. Jerry *loved* grapes which he would swallow whole and, as you might guess, everyone wanted to give him treats. We had to keep an eye on his treat intake, so not to overdo it since he was already overweight. He also loved lettuce which is much better for him and helped keep him hydrated.

Due to Jerry's weight problem, his feet stayed swollen all the time. We gave him arthritis medication to help with his discomfort. The other issue Jerry had from being overweight was with his crop. This is the area leading to the stomach where food would begin digestion. His crop had become stretched and would fill with air as he ate. Now here's the surprise, we discovered through hugging him and by gently squeezing him, we could help him *burp*! YES, we burped the turkey! It seemed a little strange and looked even stranger! We would straddle him as if we were going to ride him, but of course, never put our weight on him. Then we'd wrap our arms around him right under his neck.

Dani Dickerson, sanctuary manager, burping Jerry.

*Have You Ever Hugged a Turkey?*

Once in position, we gave him a gentle squeeze and out came burps, quite loud, I might add! You could tell he immediately felt better.

Jerry had another amazing trait; he could change the color of his head and neck! He could also draw in his snood (this is the dangly part that hangs from the top of his head). He could draw it into a short cone, or let it droop long and floppy. His neck would change from light blue to bright red, depending on whether he was cold or hot, excited or relaxed. Turkeys are amazing creatures!

Jerry with his snood drawn up in a cone which means he's concerned about something. When he lets it dangle, he's relaxed.

Several years went by and Jerry was, for sure, one of our most popular animals! People who came out for tours to meet all the animals would fall in love with our handsome boy, especially after getting a hug! There were those who always came back at Thanksgiving just to hug Jerry and tell him how much they loved him.

After several years, Jerry's body was growing weak and his feet seemed to ache all the time. We knew it was time to let him go. I hope he could see the Rainbow Bridge in the sky and other creatures that were there to greet him. Several of his human friends hugged and kissed him as he made his way to the Bridge, all of us knowing we would see each other again.

Our lives bring us many changes, but one thing stays the same, the love we feel in our hearts is real and that is the greatest gift of all!

If you're ever lucky enough to meet a turkey like Jerry who would allow you to touch him, you should definitely give him a hug!

Ashley Hedrick, mom to Emma Schneller, giving Jerry a hug.

Colton Draper came to hug Jerry every Thanksgiving.

Missy resting after therapy

# 8
# *Missy's Amazing Recovery*

In this story we see that sometimes, even when things seem hopeless, miracles can happen! Miss Belle, who we called Missy, is one of those stories. We went on a call for an infant fawn ramming herself into a fence in someone's backyard. Apparently, she and her mom had jumped the 6-foot fence to get into the yard to eat, but when the people in the house noticed them and went outside, the mom jumped back out. Missy was still so small that in her panic she couldn't muster the strength to make it over the fence. In the wild, if she were trapped in a thicket area, she could continually push until she made her way through, but this wasn't a thicket, it was a metal chain link fence!

By the time we arrived, Missy had been relentless in trying to make her way "through" the fence to get back to her mom, and she was growing very weary. We could not see her mother, but I feel sure she was in the edge of the woods, watching and hoping her baby would be okay. Terrified of humans, as she should be, it was difficult to approach her without scaring her even more. I had taken some calming oils with me. Once we got her wrapped in the blanket, I started giving them to her, and they seemed to calm her a little. We hurried to get her back to the sanctuary to a quiet space.

Once we got to SC CARES, upon examination, we realized that her neck was very swollen from continually running head first into the fence. We later confirmed with the vet that the swelling had pressed on the nerves to her spinal column causing paralysis to her extremities, which meant she could not use her legs at all! Others may have ended her life, knowing a deer that could not stand and walk

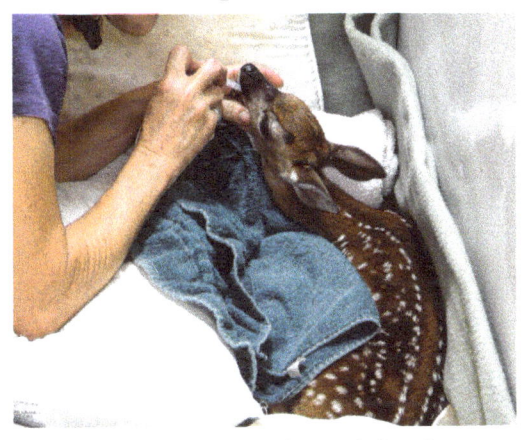

Missy when she arrived as an infant fawn. Beauty in its purest form.

Missy's Amazing Recovery

Missy's daily exercises to learn how to walk!

Cindy and a volunteer helping Missy do water therapy.

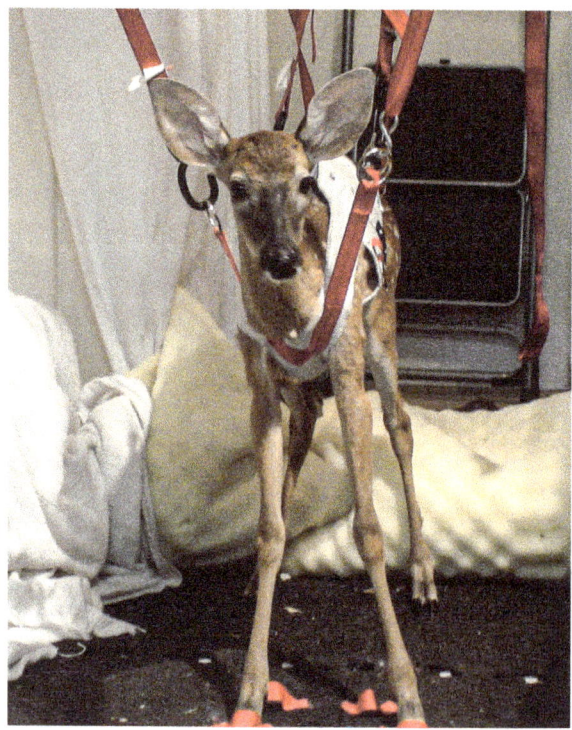

Missy in the sling that two volunteers designed and made.

*Tails from SC CARES*

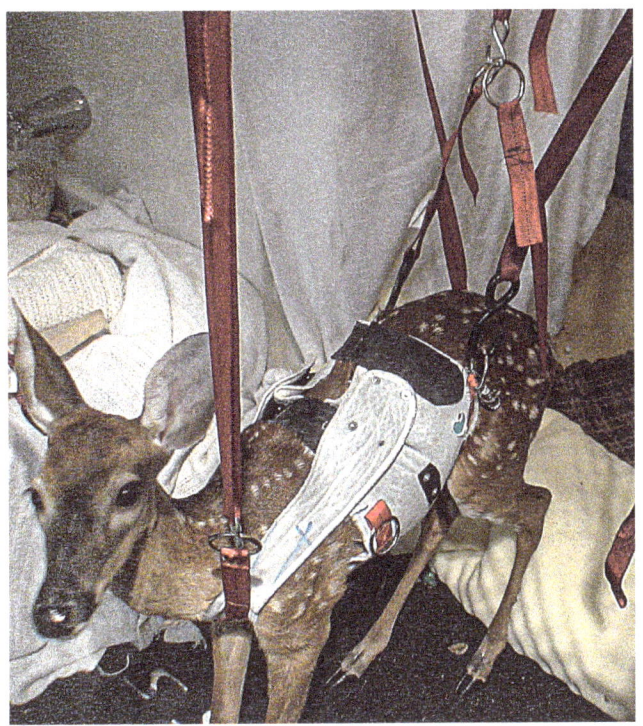

Missy in her sling to help her gain strength and mobility.

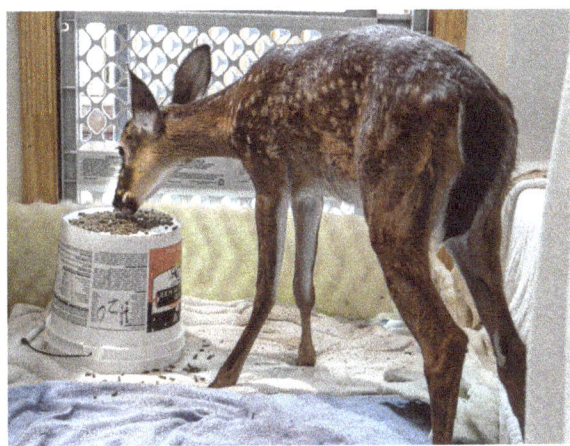

Missy finally standing on her own!

Skip's ingenious invention to keep Missy's feet from sliding out from under her. Notice the progressive placement for her as she grew.

*Missy's Amazing Recovery*

would not survive under any circumstances, but we just couldn't do it ... we had to at least give her a chance.

We began bottle feeding her, and added some immune boosting herbs to hopefully help with her injuries. I mixed some essential oils to use on her back, her neck, and each joint of all four legs. Every day, at least three times a day, I would do physical therapy on her, using the oil to massage her so she did not become stiff. Missy's recovery became the focus of all the people at SC CARES and everyone was doing their part to help her.

We were fortunate to have two volunteers who were able to be a tremendous help to Missy. One of our volunteers designed a sling to cup her body and allow her legs to hang out, and another volunteer, a great seamstress, made the sling. The sling worked perfectly! Our co-director came up with floor mats and made slits from strong material for her little hooves to fit into to help her stand. For several months, three times a day, I continued physical therapy on Missy, and we would feed her each of her bottles while she was in the sling, eventually getting some movement from her by enticing her with the bottle. We lowered the sling as she grew, so that she could put weight on her legs and build up her strength.

Missy continued to grow so another larger sling had to be made, this time with loops so that we could take her outside to teach her how to walk. I was still massaging her joints and continued to hoist her up in the sling while she took her bottle. Then, at least once a day, we took her in the sling, with poles through the sides, and went outside to let her begin to use her legs to walk. We bought a large tub that we filled with water so she could do water therapy. This helped her to use her legs without putting too much strain on them.

We were honestly shocked that she continued to show improvement. This little deer did not want to give up and neither would we! After months and months of rehab and therapy with Missy, she DID learn to walk. It wasn't as elegant as most deer, and she still had some balance issues, but she could move around on her own and could run better than she could walk.

After being completely paralyzed with not much hope, all of us including Missy, couldn't give up! Missy's will to live and all the effort and love that surrounded her helped make this happen. This just goes to show you that, if you want something bad enough and work hard at it, chances are your dreams will come true!

Missy, standing on her own. Her legs weren't exactly right, but she was able to walk and run.

Toto – we had two tortoises name Tortellini, so he was called Toto for short.

# 9
# *Our Little Dinosaurs*

At SC CARES, we cared for African Spurred Sulcata Tortoises. These magnificent creatures seemed very similar to what small dinosaurs might have been like. These tortoises are native to the desert areas in Africa and thrive in that climate. Sadly, years back, someone thought it would be profitable to bring these tortoises to the States to breed and sell them. Currently, they are in the exotic pet industry at pet stores and reptile shows. These creatures are amazing but were not meant to be pets!

These tortoises cannot swim like turtles that most of us are accustomed to seeing. However, they do enjoy soaking in a shallow tray of water, especially when it is hot outside. If you look closely at turtle and tortoise feet, you will see a big difference. The turtles have webbing between their toes, which helps them paddle through the water, making them avid swimmers. However, the tortoise feet are designed for digging and have no webbing! Their feet are solid and they have claws for toenails, which in the desert would be perfect for digging a burrow to sleep in.

Our visitors were always amazed at how fast they can move, especially when it was feeding time. To watch them from a distance, they appear to be rocks moving along the ground. According to our veterinarian, that is what a healthy tortoise should feel like as well, little boulders, and after they are about 8-10 years old, their weight should be between 30-40 pounds.

Just out for a stroll in the warmth of the sun.

Sulcata tortoises do best on dry grasses to meet their feelings of hunger. Just like humans, you really are what you eat ... if we fill up on sugary junk foods, we become overweight and sick. The tortoises are no different, and unfortunately, it has become an issue with captive-bred tortoises that are given too many fruits and veggies and are now in poor health. Their bodies are not set up to metabolize sugary, rich foods. Just as humans become

Freddie chowing down on "greens day."

unhealthy from eating too much of these foods, the tortoise's sign of being unhealthy is that they have shell deformities. You can see the difference in their shells; some end up with pyramided shells, points that are raised up, which is not how it should be. The smoother the shell, most likely the healthier the tortoise!

Speaking of the shell, another delightful fact is that these tortoises can feel our touch on their shell. For visitors at SC CARES, "tortoise tickling" was one of the more popular parts of our tour. One of our residents, a bull (male) named Sahara, was especially fond of having his bum tickled, so much so that he would do a little dance we call the "bum wiggle." It is amazing that as thick and strong as their shells are, they can feel even the slightest touch. Their shells grow as they grow; they do not shed them or remove themselves as crabs do.

In the exotic pet trade, when purchasing these creatures, most people are uninformed as to the care and longevity of this species. Most pet stores sell tortoises as hatchlings, which will fit in the palm of your hand. They are so adorable that the fascination of this creature apparently blocks out this information, if they even receive any. The fact is, within five years, this cute little creature will be upwards of 20 pounds, eating everything in sight and is NOT a candidate for being potty-trained! This will create an issue for the uninformed buyer.

So, what does one do with such a creature? He cannot live in a terrarium now, and for optimum health, he must be outside with natural sunlight and plenty of room to move about. Although these tortoises look very rugged, they are actually very delicate when it comes to

Community group and single males out to bask in the sun.

Victorious hiding – he has always been shy.

Speedy – our eldest and largest resident.

cold temperatures. They need a heat source for those cold days and nights. If a tortoise is living in temperatures 30 degrees or below for more than 48 hours, all of their organs gradually begin to slow down, until finally they all stop!

Within the first 15 years, the Sulcatas continue to grow to upwards of 100 pounds and 36" in diameter. Trust me, at this point, they go where they want to go, when they choose to. Unless you are a weight lifter, you will not be picking them up to move them. Plus, these wonderful creatures have lifespans of 80-100 years! Yes, that is right, 80-100 years, just as humans can live to be 80-100 years old. So most of the tortoises will outlive their caretakers if they are cared for properly.

All of these wonderful reptiles have such unique personalities, and our visitors were amazed to watch them and see how differently they acted. Some were bullies, while others were very shy. There are tortoises who were greeters, very friendly and wanting your attention, while others wanted to ram you! People more often do not understand that, just like all other animals, these tortoises are sentient beings. This means they have

Sebastian – up close and personal.

likes and dislikes, personalities, and they all want to be taken care of.

Lastly, if you ever happen upon someone selling "rides" on the tortoises, *please* do not do it! There is a picture of the skeleton of a tortoise and, as you can see, their bones are just big enough to carry their own weight. Adding any additional weight could break their legs! Always be kind to creatures you encounter, because they are more like US than you might realize!

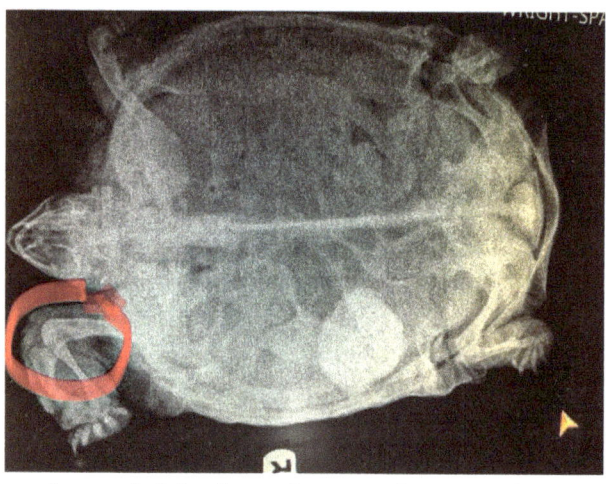

This x-ray of a tortoise's leg shows they can only support their own weight.

Abbott – one of the friendliest residents.

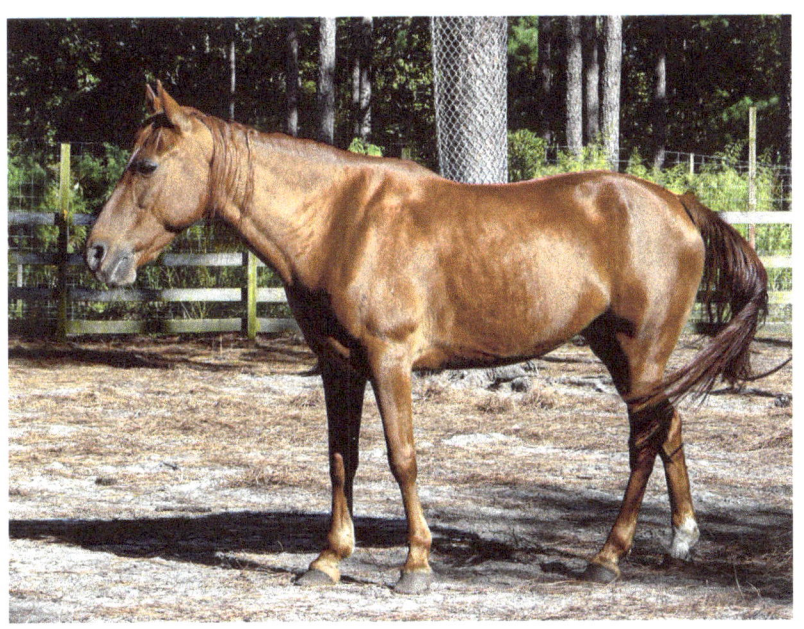

Sassy, the beautiful girl she was meant to be!

## 10

## *Sassy*

This story starts off sad but keep reading – the ending is wonderful!! This is a story of a horse who had probably lost all hope in life, and most certainly lost faith in humans. In May of 2013, concerned citizens reported animal abuse in a paddock where two horses were being kept. Upon the rescuer's arrival, she found two horses, one had already passed away from starvation, and his friend was standing over him with her head laying on his lifeless body. For that poor creature, it was too late. What makes this situation even worse is the fact that there were unopened bags of horse feed on the property, so it wasn't a matter of not having money for the food, just a lack of compassion and humanity to go out and feed them. There are no words to describe how this makes an animal rescuer feel.

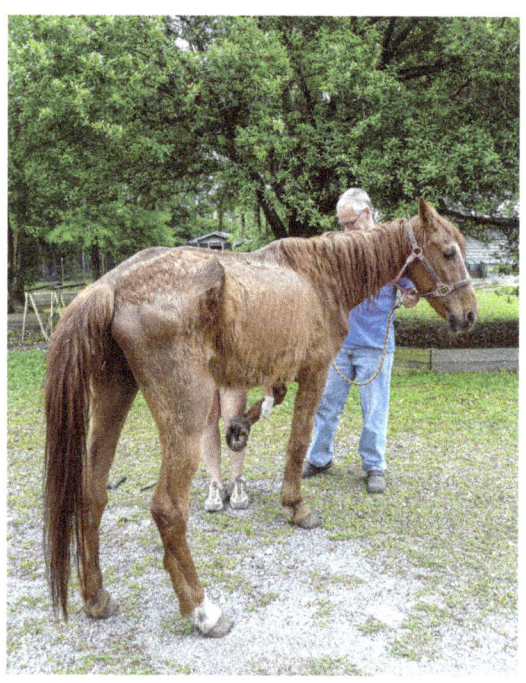

Sassy being evaluated by the vet when she arrived.

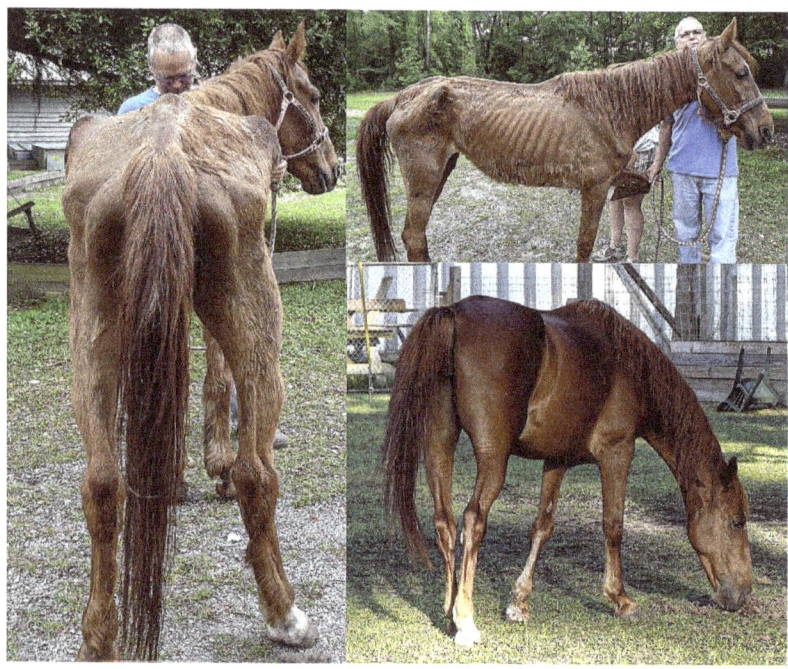

Sassy "before" and "after" she had gained a couple hundred pounds.

*Tails from SC CARES*

The surviving horse was later named Sassy (for **S**weet and **S**assy Surviving **Y**et). Against all odds and with the spirit to overcome the abuse and neglect she had been forced to endure, Sassy was brought to SC CARES and our vet was immediately called. It was so painful to see the frail skeleton of a horse being unloaded from the trailer, it took my breath away, and made me feel sick. What should be a magnificent creature had been left to die, and had watched her paddock mate suffer to his death. Horses are very close to each other in their herds (families), so in addition to her own health being compromised, her heart was hurting for her lost friend.

Once the vet arrived, she began to check everything with Sassy. She determined that Sassy was probably 6 or 7 years old. She also determined that Sassy had been without enough food to eat for over a year! Without having the food her body needed, her skeletal structure had already changed. Her front legs had grown too close together from being too skinny, making her front feet turn out (club footed). Thankfully it didn't affect her ability to move and run, but it did look a little strange. The vet also heard a heart murmur because Sassy was so thin, and to make matters even worse, Sassy had a tumor on her front foot that was cancer! This cancerous tumor could have been avoided completely if she had been cared for. Sassy apparently injured her foot some time back and the injury was left untreated, causing an infectious mass to grow, becoming cancerous. Our vet did the surgery on Sassy to remove the mass and we cleaned, dressed it and medicated it for quite some time and eventually it healed!

Horses require a lot of work to keep them healthy and happy! In addition to their food, water, and grooming, they need vaccinations, medications for worming, pedicures for their feet, and dental visits for their teeth! Just as our finger- and toenails grow, so do the horse's hooves, and for them to walk properly and without pain, their hooves must be kept trimmed. This is the job of the farrier. Unlike humans, a horse's teeth continue to grow through their lives, and will grow into points if they're not cared for. An equine vet does this job. Under sedation, with the proper tools, the horse's teeth must be filed down to remain flat. This procedure is called "floating the teeth," and if it's not done, the horse will not be able to chew and eat properly, and it could eventually cause its death. We were frequently asked about how wild horses survive without this type of care. My response was that wild horses are eating different foods, walking on different surfaces, and, I imagine, they may not have the lifespan that horses in captivity have. This is, of course, my best guess.

Now, on to the happy ending! Sassy grew stronger each day, eating and gaining the weight her body needed. Her heart murmur disappeared as she put on the hundreds of pounds she needed. Her cancer mass healed, her coat became shiny and beautiful, and she was now a healthy, happy horse! While living at SC CARES, Sassy met another horse who lived here; his name is Cupid! In just a few weeks, Cupid and Sassy became best friends, where you saw one, the other was right there! Cupid would not leave Sassy's side the entire time she was

Sassy in all her health and beauty.

Cupid and Sassy together forever.

*Sassy*

healing, and he would stand at the fence neighing, not taking his eyes off her when we had to take her out for her vet visits. He couldn't wait for her to come back to the paddock with him. The two horses formed a friendship filled with love, and they had so much fun together! Sassy thankfully had the spirit and strength to live, and we are so grateful we were able to help her regain a healthy body and find a new best friend! This is what rescue is all about!

Cupid nuzzling Sassy to say, "I love you!"

An infant opossum learning to climb before being released.

## 11
## *We Are All Important*

Wildlife Rehabilitation is an important task and very much needed. At SC CARES, our facility filled up so quickly with resident animals that, sadly, we were not able to do much wildlife rehabilitation. For various reasons, our native wildlife often end up in situations where human intervention is necessary for them to survive. An opossum momma is hit by a car, leaving her babies alone; trees are cut down with squirrels' nests in them; baby birds just learning to fly are attacked by a cat or dog, and various other reasons.

In this story, let's talk about opossums! These wonderful creatures have not received the appreciation they deserve for the purposes they serve. Opossums are the only marsupial creature in the entire North American continent. "Marsupial" means they carry their babies in a pouch near their tummies. Other marsupials are the kangaroo, koala bears, sugar gliders, wombats and many more. Nearly all but the opossum live in Australia. Humans have not been educated enough about the opossum, so here are some myth busters:

1. Opossums are highly unlikely to carry rabies because their body temperature is too low for rabies to live in them;

2. They are very relaxed creatures and do not attack unless they're cornered and have no way to escape;

3. They will not attack or eat other living creatures, like a cat or dog.

Wildlife rehabilitation takes a lot of knowledge, practice, time, and patience. When infants arrive at a rescue, the rescuer must commit to several months of care for them before they will be ready for release back into the wild. It's a very long time, especially in the beginning, when the babies need to eat every three hours, including through the night. The goal for rescuers is to get them back in the wild, so they can be free and live fulfilling lives.

Cindy feeding one of the infant opossums. This is not the most efficient way to feed them though; it's much better to tube feed.

Infant opossum – cutest little face!

Infants learning to eat solid foods.

Animals in the wild all have a purpose, or job to do. They are all part of the balance of life on earth called the ecosystem. Opossums have a huge job to do in the wild that tremendously helps us humans! Their biggest task is to help clean up their surroundings. Like the vulture, the opossum cleans up dead things. By doing this, these creatures help keep diseases from forming and making us sick! I like to call the opossum and the vulture our "garbage collectors" for the community. Opossums also eat ticks, LOTS of ticks! It is said that they can consume 5,000 ticks in a year and WOW! that's great, because none of us wants to be bitten by a tick!

At SC CARES, we had several opossums that needed to live with us. Of course, we would have rather released them in the wild, but sometimes there are circumstances that kept us from being able to do that. Medical issues and, sadly, imprinting seem to be two of the top reasons. "Imprinting" means that they became too close to humans and are not afraid enough of them to be in the wild. Well-meaning people have

Betty, held by Dani Dickerson, the sanctuary manager, at one of our animal presentations.

*Tails from SC CARES*

raised infant opossums and treated them like pets, which is not how the opossums should be raised to live safely in the wild.

Here are some more interesting facts about the opossum. Opossums are great climbers! They have a prehensile tail, which means it's very strong and they can use it to grip branches and hold on like a monkey, although they normally cannot hang by their tails because they weigh too much for their tails to hold them. They have opposable thumbs on their hind feet which help them grip better while they're climbing. Monkeys and humans have opposable thumbs, too!

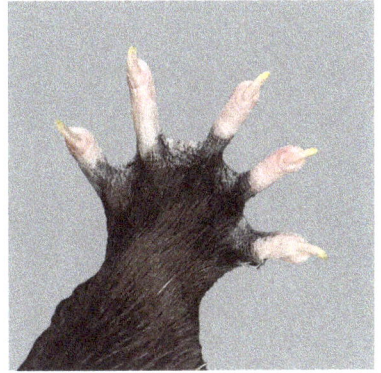

Betty's front foot. Unfortunately, we did not get a picture of the back foot.

If an opossum is threatened or becomes very scared, it can "play dead." When they do this, their bodies become very still and lifeless, and they put off an odor that smells like something dead or rotten.

Betty, a non-releasable opossum out to play.

*We Are All Important*

Humans say the phrase "playing opossum" when they're saying someone is pretending something! Opossums also have an immunity to most snake venom, meaning if they're bitten by a venomous snake, it most likely will not make them sick.

I hope this story has given you a new way to think about opossums and how wonderful and important they are. We are ALL important and have a purpose in this world. The earth will be better if we are each allowed to do our part! If you have an interest in helping wildlife, please contact your nearest Wildlife Rehabilitation Center to learn more!

This wonderful poster has been on Facebook for quite a while but no listing of who to credit for it. Whoever it is, we thank you!

Meet the pack: Anna Marie, Cira, Captain, Duchess, Calypso

# 12
# *Wolf Pack*

SC CARES was a sanctuary for ALL types of creatures, including a pack of wolves! Our wolf pack became one of the most sought-after groups of animals for our visitors. People would come to see them from all across the United States and Canada. The wolves came to SC CARES as 8-week-old pups who had been rescued from a roadside menagerie that was known to sell exotic animals to the public. The situation of wolves in private homes usually results in tragedy for the wolf. In so many cases, these wolves and wolf dogs are sold to people who think they can keep the wolf as a companion animal; sadly, too often the wolf's instincts don't make that situation a safe scenario. In addition to safety issues, the wolves are not given the opportunity to live happy lives.

Of course, our wish would be for all wolves to live in the wild where they can thrive but, in some cases, when that's not a possibility, a sanctuary is an alternative.

The SC CARES wolf pack was bred between an Alaskan wolf (mother) and a British Columbian wolf (father) which is why three of the wolves are predominately white and the remaining two are black. In 2006, when they arrived as 8-week-old pups, Skip and I worked with them hands-on every day for months. We wanted them to be social so we could work with them more comfortably. After several months, we were seeing no

With the stress of change, the wolf pups' tummies were upset, which is why we were bathing Captain Jack (left) and Calypso (right) to clean them.

progress with their feeling comfortable with us, so we decided that their wild instincts were more powerful than we could overcome. It was not fair to them and selfish of us to cause them such stress each day and make no headway, so we just allowed them to be wolves.

Wolves instinctively have a hierarchy (order) in the pack, and this bond is stronger than we can ever understand. Their connection to each other in this hierarchy seems stronger than any human family could ever be.

For wolves to survive in the wild, the hierarchy must be followed with committed respect. In a pack of wolves, there is an alpha male, alpha female, betas, and omegas. This order is an astonishing and complex system.

Full-blooded wolf pups at 2 months old (above) and 5 months old (below).

In the wild, the alphas would be the only wolves to breed, and these two would be the hunters responsible for finding food for the entire pack. When food was captured, the alphas would eat their fill before the rest of the pack could approach the meal. This helps ensure their survival as the lead wolves. The pack decides who is strong enough and smart enough to take this position.

*Wolf Pack*

The dominance trials are all tests that each individual wolf will carry out to test that leader and make sure they're qualified to protect and care for the pack.

Next in order is the beta, somewhat like the middle child. Their responsibility is to help care for the young pups when they're born, a nanny, so to speak, while the alphas are out hunting. The betas also have a very important job in the hierarchy of the pack, and that's to help maintain order. They're often referred to as the clowns of the pack – if a situation is getting too heated, the betas' responsibility is to create a distraction, to cause a pause in the feud, so that no member of the pack is gravely injured. Finally, there are the omegas at the bottom of the hierarchy in the pack. This does not mean they aren't important. The omega must constantly submit to his fellow pack members and are sometimes persecuted by them or treated as a scapegoat. However, omegas often take the initiative in play, thus helping to ease tensions in the pack.

When our pack arrived, they had already been given names, Captain Jack, Duchess, Cira, Calypso, and Anna Marie. Captain was the only male and brother to his four sisters, so by default he was the alpha male! Originally as pups, Calypso was the alpha female, and we knew this because, when we approached the pack, the others would go behind Captain and Calypso, leaving them in front as their protectors. This position changed when the girls reached their second birthday, and although Duchess was the smallest, she became the alpha female and retained that position for the remainder of their lives.

Captain Jack (above), alpha male, and Duchess (below), alpha female.

Just goes to show you it's not about size, it's more about attitude! Cira was the beta, the "enforcer," as I liked to call her! She was not so much a clown as she seemed to be more like a general, keeping all things in order! She would play with the alphas and the omegas but never at the same time. Lastly, we have the omegas who were Calypso and Anna Marie. These two were often seen lying together, and at feeding time, were beside each other for dinner.

Cira (above), beta

Calypso (lower left), omega
Anna Marie (lower right), omega

One of the few pictures of all five wolves together. (Left to right) Captain, Cira, Anna Marie, Duchess and Calypso.

Captain Jack rubbing Cindy's hand to pick up her scent and sniffing Skip's scent.

*Wolf Pack*

These wolves each had its own special personality, and we are so grateful we were able to share our lives with them and learn so much! We were very fortunate to find a wolf biologist, Jeremy Heft, who had studied wolf behavior for years, and he was remarkable at helping us understand our wolf pack. His advice enabled us to give our wolves the safest and best life we could offer them in captivity.

Since we lived on the property, we essentially lived with the wolves! It was a wonderful experience to share their lives for more than 13 years! Wolves are majestic and mysterious creatures. There were a lot of evenings that the pack would howl, so harmoniously and so beautifully! Their song would make you stop in your tracks, and you would become mesmerized by the sound. Full blooded wolves don't bark, they may chuff (like a tiger), but never bark, so howling is their way of vocalizing!

Within the pack, they communicated with each other in many other ways, ear placement, stance and body direction, and if they really wanted the attention, growl. If we ever heard a strange noise that we needed to investigate, as soon as we stepped outside, we could look at the

Looking beautiful while howling and sounding remarkable!

wolves to see what direction it came from. They were always alert and knew exactly what was going on around them. We're so grateful to share our lives with these wolves and will treasure our experience forever!

Four of the five wolves being lazy on a spring morning. (Left to right) Cira, Duchess, Calypso and Captain Jack.

*Wolf Pack*

## 13
## *A Cat Named "Mayo"*

My name at first, I did not know,
as I spent my days wandering to and fro.
On one of my journeys, I found an old jar,
and I was so hungry because I'd traveled so far!

So, I licked, and I licked and pushed my head inside
then my head wouldn't come out – believe me, I tried!
My head was now stuck with this jar on top,
I tried hard to free myself, I even jumped and hopped!

Oh, I hate this has happened! Oh what will I do?
I had to think of a plan, and quickly, too!
So I climbed a fence to the very top,
in hopes someone might see me and stop!

At last a lady came to help me,
I was really hoping she could get my head free!
When the lady finally got me, I wiggled and squirmed,
I must have felt like a wet, squiggly worm!

The lady and her friend held on to me tight,
and they pulled and pulled with all their might!
The jar finally came off, oh, what a relief,
I sure wish humans would stop littering – good grief!

Now that the jar was off I could rest,
and these people gave me a bed that was the best!
For the next few days I was fed, and I was loved,
it felt so good I thought I'd died and gone above!

This was all great but OH! wait – it's not the end,
I met new people who would be my best friends!
I suppose I am fortunate that jar got stuck
since it really changed my life's luck!

I live with my new mom and dad and new brother dog!
We run, we play, we eat – then sleep like a log!
My life is wonderful! I smile from ear to ear.
I'm the luckiest cat ever and so glad to be here!

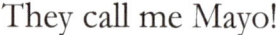

They call me Mayo!

*Illustrations by my very talented niece, Bella Cabrera!*

Poor kitty, when we found her with a plastic mayonnaise jar stuck on her head!

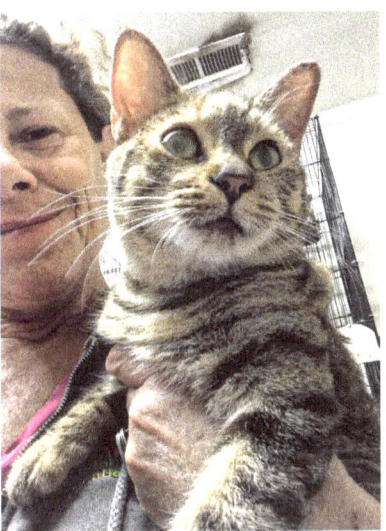

Mayo – so happy to be fed, safe and loved!

Mayo and her sweet brother Shadow in their forever home!

*A Cat Named "Mayo"*

## Words used in Tails from SC CARES

**Alpha** – Socially dominant, especially in a group

**Beta** – Second in position or ranking

**Bond** – To form a close relationship with

**Compassion** – To be sympathetic, care for and want to help all living creatures

**Crop** – Pouch located under a bird's throat where food begins to digest

**Dominant** – Commanding, controlling; in a superior position

**Earthquaking** – Shaking a bird's cage so rapidly the bird falls off its perch

**Equine** – Relating to a horse

**Exotic** – Not native to the area they're in; from another country

**Farrier** – A person who shoes horses and cares for their feet

**Floating the teeth** – Term used by equine veterinarians to describe filing teeth flat

**Fortitude** – Strength of mind to encounter pain and danger with courage

**Harlequin** – A bird bred by a Blue & Gold and a Green-winged macaw

**Hierarchy** – An order of ranking

**High content** – Greater degree of wolf in a wolf/dog mixed breed DNA

**Imprinting** – Learned behavior, often bonding to someone other than normal

**Intimidating** – Producing feelings of fear, causing lack of self-confidence

**Kindred spirits** – Like-minded beings that have an instant understanding, connection

## *and what they mean*

**Marsupial** – A female mammal whose body has a pouch to carry their young

**Menagerie** – A collection of various animals, usually for exhibition

**Metabolize** – The process of the body to break down food and convert it to energy

**Non-releasable** – Not able to be set free

**Omega** – The lowest class of a hierarchy; the submissive class

**Paddock** – An enclosed area for animals, often refers to horses

**Preening** – To groom and smooth feathers

**Prehensile** – The ability of a body part to grasp and hold objects

**Quonset** – A prefabricated, corrugated structure usually with an arching roof

**Rainbow Bridge** – A term to describe the place our animal friends' spirits go to wait to see us again (heaven)

**Raptors** – Meat-eating birds that use their strong feet with sharp talons (nails) to hunt

**Rehabilitation** – The process of healing and restoring the body

**Sanctuary** – A place of refuge and protection

**Self-mutilate** – The act of causing harm or injury to oneself

**Sentient** – The ability to perceive or feel things; able to feel emotions and have distinct personalities

**Snood** – The fleshy part on a turkey above the beak

**Terrarium** – Usually a glass enclosure to house small animals indoors

**Wolf hybrid** – Wolves who have been bred with dogs

## Sanctuaries that helped SC CARES

Wild Things – https://wildthingsfc.org/ https://www.facebook.com/wildlifefreedom1/
Hope Acres – http://www.hopeacresrescue.org
Angel Winds Sanctuary – https://www.facebook.com/Angel-Winds-Horse-Sanctuary-283703662309798/
The Pig Preserve – https://linktr.ee/thepigpreserve
Whispering Rise Farm – http://www.wrfas.org
Flip Side Sanctuary – https://linktr.ee/flip_side_sanctuary
Charlie's Harmony Sanctuary – https://www.facebook.com/Charlies-Harmony-Sanctuary-Farm-1114675092046873/
Big Oak Wolf Sanctuary – http://www.bigoakwolfsanctuary.org
Valiant Animal Rescue – http://www.ValiantAnimalRescue.org
Izzie's Pond – http://www.izziespond.org
Wild Things Preserve – https://www.facebook.com/WildThingsPreserve/
Gainesville Rabbit Rescue – http://www.gainesvillerabbitrescue.org
Metropolitan Guinea Pig Rescue – http://www.mgpr.org
Noah's Ark Animal Sanctuary – http://www.noahs-ark.org
Papayago House Rescue – http://www.papayagorescuehouse.org
Ziggy's Haven Bird Sanctuary – http://www.ziggyshaven.org
Rescue Ranch – http://www.rescueranch.com
The Oasis Sanctuary – http://www.the-oasis.org
A Helping Wing Parrot Rescue – http://www.ahelpingwing.org

## Acknowledgment

My sincere thanks to the CLASS Publishing team –
Linda Ketron, Editor & Publisher,
Anne Malarich, Photography Editor,
Charlene McSweeny, Graphic Designer,
D'Ann O'Donovan & Annie Pott, Copy Editors –
for bringing this dream to reality.

~CH

www.ingramcontent.com/pod-product-compliance
Lightning Source LLC
Chambersburg PA
CBHW061745290426
43673CB00095B/269